Kosmokrator

Kosmokrator, Volume 1

Yperion Press

Published by Yperion Press, 2024.

While every precaution has been taken in the preparation of this book, the publisher assumes no responsibility for errors or omissions, or for damages resulting from the use of the information contained herein.

KOSMOKRATOR

First edition. March 19, 2024.

Copyright © 2024 Yperion Press.

ISBN: 979-8224119707

Written by Yperion Press.

Whoever declares himself to be God,
let him come and finish this corner,
and then all shall know he is a god.

Introduction

Kosmokrator was created with the intention to communicate to like-minded or simply curious individuals the different avenues through which they may acquire personal power and knowledge of the world. In using this phrasing we must introduce important caveats. First, that we do not mean what others do when using these words. Second, that our notions of what power entails are more nuanced but may include the more monolithic notion of it as a form of control.

By power we refer to Richard Bandler's notion of having a choice. This very functional definition of what power consists is at the most elementary and easily comprehensible level gives us a much more flexible and *useful* concept to work with. It also gives us a direction. When you feel powerless in a situation, by looking around you can quickly come to realize that what you are lacking are options. Therefore, the acquisition of power consists in either developing new ways of thinking and acting, or in becoming aware of what was available there altogether.

By world we refer to everything that you can experience. Your own world includes thoughts, emotions, impressions, on any and all events, subjects and objects, or whatever words you use to identify the elements of your entire experience of being alive.

Kosmokrator aims to explore the fringes of said power, and shall touch on a variety of topics bordering on what has hitherto been problematically called the "paranormal". To achieve depth, however, we have decided to center our main efforts around concrete practices that any individual may replicate and practice in their own private setting.

Aim and Scope

Our publication has as its centerpiece two practices: that of remote viewing, and that of the out-of-body experience. Discussions will go around, and well beyond these two topics, but these will be the visible secular disciplines to develop in order to turn research and speculation into profound explorations stretching the boundaries of what you thought could be known.

Remote viewing consists of the methodical and analytical process through which one can access progressively deeper levels of intuition. The feasibility of said process for military and commercial intelligence have been ascertained and are not, for those operating professionally and earning a living within the field, in doubt. Because remote viewing relies entirely on the conscious-unconscious connection but is also put under the pressure of a strict protocol, it is equal parts an art (or, some would say, martial art) as well as a science.

The out-of-body experience is exactly what its name describes: the reported account of individuals that consciousness can function outside the limitations of the physical body. Whether that occurs in actuality *outside* of the body, in the mind where a map of reality exists, or whether *the universal mind* that encompasses all individual minds is the scene where such events unfold, is a matter of metaphysical discussion and only peripheral to our intent. The metaphysical matter is, in short, not our priority. What matters most to us is the seeking, having, and dominating of the experience.

Assumptions

We assume that you are truly interested in what is termed esoteric development, but really just amounts to existential expansion. We also assume that you will acquire and engage with our publications on a continual basis and in the sequential order in which they appear. The reason for this is that we shall progressively delve deeper into the practical aspects surrounding the suggested activities. It is entirely possible that discussions down the line shall assume knowledge of topics previously discussed. We may even come to assume that the reader has reached a certain level of proficiency in the outlined disciplines so that anything we put down on paper has a direct and immediate application to those it reaches.

We do not assume, but we would prefer it, if the people engaging with our literature would also engage in physically demanding disciplines. Doing so rounds off the person, roots out certain personality traits, and reinforces the central motor of any endeavor, that of the Will.

All that said, anyone is free to read for educational purposes alone. Every person decides how they will engage with the material, if they will definitely be serious and dedicated to following us and our publications, and assume total responsibility for their own actions and chosen methods. What we share here are internal notes on our own practices and interests.

Justification

Having remote viewing and the out-of-body experience as central practices requires a host of other skills to be trained in parallel. That is, these skills are composite or complex processes resulting from a multitude of converging abilities each of which require discipline to develop. When approached naturally, or when trained systematically, the point can be reached where they are a singular (or single-event) abilities. Children can spontaneously develop the ability to consciously dream and seemingly leave their physical locations without their physical bodies. These states are also most commonly associated with spontaneous visionary abilities.

As such, these two abilities are both a return to a kind of birthright for our species, and also an exploration and development of the furthest reaches of our existential capacity from our current general vantage point. We have chosen each for a very specific reason.

The importance of remote viewing lies in the ability to acquire detailed information anytime and anywhere about any event taking place anytime and anywhere else. The metaphysical reasons or implications are, to us, less important than the already established fact that this has been practically demonstrated in laboratory and field conditions. It is a revolutionary skill in accessing information available to any normally functioning human being.

The out-of-body experience, for its own part, offers the most immersive and mind-bending experience that humans have access to without endangering limb or life. It has been described as more *real* than the physical experience. More real here, we interpret by reading such claims in detail, as meaning more intense and focused. While remote viewing is about precision in data collection, the out-of-body experience is about richness and variation, leading to enhanced pleasure and learning.

Focusing on these two practices gives us the tools of an expanded awareness and experience with which to probe deeper into investigations related to historical, high-profile, or other events of interest. The more involved, technically speaking, is remote viewing. Achieving the out-of-body experience, on the other hand, while subject to the use of techniques, tends to rely a lot more on instinct and pure sensation. Thus, there will be much more to discuss, in general, in the exploration of remote viewing. After all, remote viewing was created for technical data collection.

Expected Levels of Development

The following is a projected sequence of levels for the development of skill. They are not meant as rules set in stone, nor as honorifics, but rather as milestones. These milestones help the progressing student focus on what most matters at their level instead of worrying about ultimate perfection, allowing each person to remain aware of what lies in front of them.

Level 1

The role of the first-entry student in any field is to become acquainted with general definitions and the proposed standards of practice of whatever institution the protocols and stipulations of which they have decided to adhere to. If, upon acquiring further familiarity with said institution, the student finds they are not compatible for any reason at all, they should be free to change to one that resonates more closely with them.

Initially the novitiate shall learn the simplest version of a technique that allows them to practice often and without great strain. Frequency and relaxation will be the order of the day. The technique used, and the expectation set, should inspire and give the novitiate a realistic but also positive feeling that fosters curiosity.

In the case of remote viewing, Level 1 practice consists of acquiring an unknown (but easily verifiable) target and quickly sketching an impression of what it might be in a matter of seconds. Doing this will release expectation and get the person used to simply doing. This practice is not aimed at high-level precision nor detail, but simply to get the conscious and unconscious into the habit, and to develop the link between them.

In the case of the out-of-body experience, a useful first skill to get used to applying is to remember to remain relaxed, immobile and aware when waking up from sleep. The state in which you will find yourself at that moment is hypnagogic. When in that state, it is quite common to experience inklings of a different aspect of reality.

Level 2

We recognize the second level has been reached because the basic techniques start to yield more than can be handled with the instructions received until this point. A certain extension and richness will be perceived that requires curiosity and bravery to explore, and open-mindedness to receive.

In remote viewing, the simple quick sketches will also become accompanied by more feelings or sensations that need descriptors beyond ideograms (doodles) hastily scribbled on paper. Here, then, the practitioner starts to understand the importance of higher levels of discipline and learning to control and organize incoming perceptions.

The second level on the road to the out-of-body experience arrives when the practitioner can consistently identify that moment when he is in a middle-state, dreaming but awake, or awake but dreaming. This can happen inside the dream (also known as lucid dreaming), or upon waking and being receptive to visual and audio patterns out of the ordinary that vanish with the onset of the complete waking state.

If lucky, the person may find themselves occasionally in an ultra-realistic and quite evident out-of-body setting. The task now will not to try and extend this state, which often leads to desperation and disorientation, but rather to *anchor* the experienced state by focusing on interacting with the perceived surroundings with the senses of sight, hearing, and touch.

Level 3

This level is all about navigating the effects of a longer operation. In remote viewing this implies a greater involvement (or interference) of the conscious with the data received. Systematic approaches to the art of distinguishing the creative faculty of mind from incoming information are necessary. This also implies a certain measure of emotional control and increased discernment above all.

In the out-of-body, stabilizing and extending the experience present formidable challenges to newcomers. Stability implies all you might think it does: the calming down of emotions, extended natural focus on the present unfolding of events. In both disciplines, this is the stage that begins to separate the casual interlopers from the serious practitioners.

Level 4

Basic dominion. What marks this level is the stabilization and clarity of the data produced through remote viewing and the events lived in the out-of-body experience. Here, both disciplines require the practitioner to understand and use certain techniques and be very aware of optimal and sub-optimal paths to success in their operations, at least in the general case.

The task of the developing remote viewer is to look in more detail into conceptual relations, abstract ideas present at the target, and other less tangible elements. The increase in accuracy and detail of the visual aspects will also be noticeable.

The task of the practitioner in the out-of-body experience is to experiment with and dominate translocation: moving to desired locations even if you do not know how to get there "physically". This opens the door to finding objects and people as well.

Higher Levels

Further and indefinite levels of control and richness seem to be possible, but these levels are what concern us at the moment. The journey there will take continual practice, study, and keeping in mind the importance of sustainable daily experience. Reports from practitioners regarding the furthest reaches of practice reveal that the lines of what a normal human being considers reality and established fact start to erode. This, however, only comes with diligent application, and a flexibility of mind.

Relinquishing control in favor of exploration

Adopting the Feldenkrais philosophy of learning has been one of the most potent additions to our arsenal of heuristics. From the outside, this might seem like choosing the easier path, avoiding effort, and so on. From the inside, what Feldenkrais advocates, at least in our view, is personalized optimization of effort and direction.

Let us explore this idea in more detail.

The way we tend to view learning in our society matches how we see work and life in general: as something to be suffered through, as if it were pain that bestowed merit. We are told as we grow up that one must make the effort, the greatest effort possible, and that eventually things will seem easy. Rewards, as it were, only come from surmounting mountains. The valley of shadow and death cannot be avoided. Such is the main narrative of our society with regards to all accomplishment.

Feldenkrais saw things differently. He thought that not only was it kinder to each person to allow them to learn at their own pace, but that doing so would, in the long run, make the person more proficient in the skill. In all this, we find an honoring of the human's animal instincts. Pain is there for a reason, and so is pleasure. Yes, we must seek not to be slaves to them, but they are assets, signals that connect us to the realities of the world of sensation.

There were several reasons for this. Feldenkrais himself made it clear that his philosophy of learning is to be applied while learning, and not in situations of emergency. There is a time to force yourself to perform beyond current levels of capacity, and that is when life has given you no alternative but to do so. However, not only is this not sustainable in the long run, it is not the most efficient approach to learning.

A child can learn to swim by being thrown in the water without warning. Or they can drown. Usually they are pulled out before they do. Oftentimes, too, traumas are codified into their nervous system by being subjected to such methods of learning. Again, it is one thing to be ready and disposed to act past your limits when the occasion arises. It is quite another to push your nervous system into a permanent state state of over excitement prone to chronic illness and shortsighted decision making.

Before we go over the tenets of what Feldenkrais called "Learning to Learn", we must emphasize again that he was not against strengthening one's capacity through exertion, nor was he averse to the idea of being ready to act well beyond one's comfort zone when in a state of emergency. Any words or ideas forthcoming must be taken as optimizations of the process of learning as it pertains to the individual as a unique system—or, as Bandler and Grinder, of Neurolinguistic Programming fame, later put it, the individual as a process and not a static thing.

To begin with, Feldenkrais advocated that, when learning, the student proceed slowly. Very slowly. Slow in the act of doing whatever it is they must learn. This does not mean that progress will of necessity come slowly, although it may. Many times, doing everything slowly results in a smoother, and thus faster, rate of absorption and a higher development of skill.

More controversially, and against the rules of engagement of our currently unhinged society, Feldenkrais stated as his second learning tenet that one should look for the pleasant sensation. Imagine that, learning without suffering, without seeking the feeling of pain, avoiding bashing one's brain against the stark wall of our limitations. There is here an honoring of the senses, that the incredible machine that is the human body has its signals for a reason. Yes, they may be poorly trained, used as an organism can become to bad habits. Another way to look at a weak body, a low tolerance for stress, is that the organism in such a state has accumulated damage. To become more resilient, and stronger, the road lies in healing and learning to walk the minefield of inputs that is the world. Such a road must be chosen and braved, and the most accurate compass is the pleasant sensation. A uniquely gauged compass for each individual. Care must be taken that this does not mean indulgence, or at least not purely. Looking for the pleasant sensation is a rule in the service of the path of learning a chosen skill, and should not become an excuse to get off the path.

From then on, Feldenkrais tells us that, when learning to do something, one should not strive to do something "nicely" nor "well". The focus of our efforts should instead be in exploration. In doing what one does slowly, with sensory awareness, attention to detail, a sense of curiosity, devoid of the conviction that one must do well, that one must achieve anything. Improvement, we can surmise from this, comes from knowing experience. But this getting-to-know through experience is best acquired by an attentive exploration, not minding perceived faults or imperfections. Above all, we may see this rule as avoiding an emphasis on imitation, where the beginner lacks the insight and familiarity necessary to correctly adapt what is seen in another, more experienced, practitioner.

But perhaps the greatest transgression against the modern ideology that makes of pain and suffering requisites is that a sense of lightness and ease should be sought out above all else. Feldenkrais entreats the learner to relax and allow detailed perceptions to differentiate input-output relations that dictate the direction to be taken. It is not trying hard that brings about learning, but finding the way that works, that "clicks", which comes about independently of whether one has tried hard or not. If we allow ourselves to explore the reasons behind the conflation of trying hard with success, we find that those said to not have tried hard enough could owe their lack of success to other factors. Not trying hard enough often means giving up too early. Many times it is a lack of focus, a lack of interest. Under these all is a lack of a sense of pleasure that comes from lightness and ease, which in turn usually make for a smooth exploratory experience that welcomes curiosity and playfulness.

Further along Feldenkrais' postulates, or recommendations, regarding learning, things turn a bit esoteric, in the best sense possible. He recommends not concentrating, but rather doing things while maintaining awareness of the world around. This favors a naturalistic flow, remaining aware of the feeling of the body, without which the signals of pain and pleasure, hardness or lightness, cannot come through clearly. But beyond that, we may add on our own, learning and doing, as a general rule, should *not* come at the expense of life itself; not even momentarily. Investigation into how mental processes affect the wider physiology of the whole bodily system would support the idea that in the midst of any activity we should maintain an awareness of the senses, internal and external. Focusing properly on an activity would then resemble the way the eye perceives incoming light, with a principal point of awareness alongside peripheral vision. The metaphor ends where the complexity of details one needs to be aware of diversify beyond mere visual awareness.

The last two rules for learning by Feldenkrais are the subtle apex of the approach. Subtle because they cannot be correctly comprehended without a nuanced approach to the rules that come before, or without direct thoughtful experience of them. The first of these last rules states that we should not, at the start of our learning experience or session, try to determine what the end state will be. The second says that we should do "a little less" than we can. The first concerns the fact that beginners tend to have a retinue of ideas about what the end result is which do not match the reality of an experienced practitioner, in whatever field of endeavor. The second aims, outwardly, at preserving the quality of the learning, of the practice; inwardly, it aims at pairing the activity with a pleasant and favorable physiology in the body.

Feldenkrais' guidelines for learning are applicable to any field. They are high level directives that, when applied conscientiously, guide the practitioner into a constant state of doing guided by curiosity, and attentive to individual limits when it comes to stamina and health, as well as creativity and capacity.

The beginning of this practice is curiosity and a lack of concern for what is considered appropriate by other parties, or by oneself. It is carried forward unencumbered by aesthetic considerations and instead opens up avenues that are favorable to the differentiated tendencies of the person. Particularly, the idea of following the pleasant sensation is conducive to high productivity. A caveat here is that we talk here of a directed search for the pleasant sensation. A looking for the pleasant sensation within the activity selected for improvement. Because the activity will always be started, continued and stopped with the correct physiology in mind, a self-reinforcing cycle will be created that will only grow stronger and more capable with the accumulation of further experience.

The Furthest Reaches

In investigating the expected levels of development of remote viewing and the out-of-body experience beyond the basic learning levels one comes to observe a convergence in the act of being, observing, acting, and living. At some point at the very elite levels of development, these skills which from the very beginning strike us as inhabiting the paranormal, but which are defined along lines that any human being can well imagine, start to cross over into less definable, godlike territory.

The phenomenon is not unique to these disciplines and has been reported in the very advanced stages of traditional martial arts, empathetic approaches to animal rearing, in the *beaux arts*, and, to a lesser extent, among writers of literature. A drastic increase in what Carl Gustav Jung referred to as synchronicity starts to take place. Premonition becomes common place, spontaneous knowledge is received of things that ought not to be known, and one develops insight into and the power to influence other beings at will nonphysically.

Joseph McMoneagle

Joseph McMoneagle as well as people who have interacted with him report his ability to communicate telepathically and to read minds. In truth, it has been reported specifically by others and only acknowledged by him as the kind of ability that advanced remote viewers in general start to find comes naturally in themselves after a certain point of development.

In defining a preliminary benchmark for what the budding remote viewer can expect when arriving at deeper and deeper levels of skill, McMoneagle touches on the increasingly alien landscape that starts to become apparent. The only thing that stops development at the very advanced levels, he specifies, is the inability of the remote viewer to reconcile the reality that unfolds before them with their models of the world (or with the staunch philosophical positions they adhere to).

Robert Allan Monroe

More commonly known as simply Robert A. Monroe, this educator and researcher of the out-of-body experience in the modern secular sphere published a trilogy of books on his gradual development of this skill and his exploration of other dimensions. Many useful things can be gleamed from his books, including techniques and curious space-time features that open up operational possibilities down the road.

Towards the very end of the trilogy, Monroe unveils more and more of what on the surface appear as less exciting, or less awe-striking features of his experience, from the point of view of the person who is most excited by the prospect of exploring *other worlds* above anything else. Nevertheless, these consist in exactly the same things Joseph McMoneagle encountered in his remote viewing journey. Telepathy, mind-reading, future-knowing, and perhaps even something akin to time-travel or remote influencing across time and space.

Madame Blavatsky

In her critically acclaimed yet terribly misunderstood masterpiece, *The Secret Doctrine*, Blavatsky sets out to unveil, in almost impossible detail, the esoteric processes by which reality has come to be and how it continues to unfold. She taps into various traditions, most emphatically Vedanta (which she favors for its liberating tendencies) and Judaism (which she, in the end, deplores for its overtones). The wording is dense and the story-telling over-extended, a sign perhaps of confusion and attachment to concepts. On the other hand, and just as a side note, the richness of analogy Blavatsky engaged in came from a vast knowledge of symbol and meaning, and so its transmission also encodes much even as it hides.

One of the features of evolution through reality that Blavatsky highlights is that she had gleamed from esoteric Buddhism that our evolution resembled an upside down bell. It had started in the subtle realms, become more and more tangible and fixed until matter was produced, and then curved upward again into the subtle, not returning whence it had come, but rather opening up a new path, new possibilities.

Consideration of this model is useful to keep in mind when encountering the weirder fringes of remote viewing and the out-of-body experience, not to mention where some physicists tell us the data regarding reality points to.

Among other things, we must notice that rather than a curse, the creating and fixing of grosser matter, also known as *the fall* in the early modern Western mythic model, was an enrichment of experience, a discovery of possibilities, a *learning*, if you will, perhaps enabling consciousness either more advanced or more nuanced operations than previously possible. It may be possible that the experience of individuality in particular is a result of this experiment. The Fall, the incursion into Hell, it would appear, while risky, promises the greatest of all bounties: consciousness strengthened to its limits, self-awareness and self-knowledge, and individual agency and freedom.

The Key Lies in Sensing

Contrary to the mainstream trend of accessing altered states through drugs and sensory deprivation, the great masters of what is called spiritual advancement, as well as the psi/paranormal/occult power geniuses of the secular modern age, the way to mastery of reality lies in enhanced awareness and an unparalleled attention to the data fed to our consciousness through direct sensations.

There have been many who think therefore that the path is too long, too difficult, or that it requires shocks to the nervous system and the psyche, using trauma as the main door. Certainly, there exists plenty of evidence for the existence of such a tradition. Nevertheless, extant sources and living practitioners also point in the direction of a smoother and faster road that does not require such self-violence. The surmounting of the thorns of the personality as a master of decision must take place, as well as the familiarity with extended sensations, a full out indulgence, even super-sensitivity to love and hate, delight and disgust, with the strength of will to dominate them.

While the doctrines of renunciation typical of the East preach separation and abandonment, and a return to some source, the authentic tradition of the West reminds us that we seek to be heroes, fools, adventurers, rascals, knights and rebels without a cause. The reason for this is simply living for its own sake. To extend our roots down to hell, and our branches to the high heavens.

Primary Practices

Correctly choosing the primary practices is an area of concern for anyone seeking to develop their overall capacities; by this we mean those of us seeking breakthroughs in the nature of human capacity itself above what is popularly touted as elite in sports or scholarly achievement. The primary practices would perhaps be different for people at different stages in their life, but not for reasons of social expectation.

Within the circles of people like us, who seek attainment beyond what is mundane or merely human, there is no separating the old from the young. On the contrary, what we may find to be primary practices are certainly largely overlooked in conventional education and culture so that young people would benefit from them as much as the old. Nevertheless, because we are agents rebelling against the overarching education and culture, we may also be taking for granted the positive aspects and skills we have developed as a result of having been brought up inside the system.

First suggestions

Any practice that aims at the total development of the human element must take into account both the physical encasing in which we exist, and the non-physical element. For those of a materialistic bent, the term non-physical need not mean soul or ethereal force in any religious or esoteric sense. The nonphysical element of the human being refers simply to the experienced reality of our identity not being coeval with the body, either in part or in whole. Nobody experiences themselves as the brain nor even the nervous system.

This is why we talk about the body and its parts as *belonging* to us, as material possessions. Fans of by-now-debunked linguistic theories might want to argue that we think this way as a result of linguistic patterns we use. Unfortunately, this language-as-primary theory has taken root in the education system even as neuroscientists (or any person with the capacity for independent judgment) had early on realized it was invalid. One only has to look at the fact that no human group, no matter the language they use, will identify the individual with the body.

As a side note, identification of thinking with language, and of individual identity with the body, which go hand in hand, is a thin construct defended by a tiny minority of people bent on making strict materialism the dominant worldview. Like all imposed worldviews against the way of truth they suffer a common obstacle: if you try to impose something false, the falsehood will fail to take root completely, and old notions will keep growing anew everywhere like weeds in the garden of deception. It is precisely this that makes necessary the huge indoctrination machine extant in most developed countries. Against such fairy tales in all realms of knowledge, truth keeps propping up when *you pay attention to your senses* instead of looking for meaning or correctness according to a given framework or model.

With regards to physical disciplines, the body needs sleep, water, nutrition, recurrent exposure to sun and open spaces (both for eye and brain health), short bouts of strain when strength is exercised, and, most elusively, *correct use*. Correct use refers to proper movement patterns and coordination. These depend on a simple understanding of joint and muscle structure, pausing between activities to allow the nervous system to reset, and in the all-too-overlooked *listening to the body*. Listening to the body is very simple: if it hurts, if it is uncomfortable, it is probably wrong (in this instance, at this time, in such a way, etc.). Listening to the body applies directly to all of the physical disciplines as well as to the nonphysical ones.

The beginning of all nonphysical discipline is, of necessity, nervous system discipline. At its most basic level is the ability to be non-reactive, as much as possible. Choosing to remain silent, immobile, despite input from the surrounding environment and the mind. Willing not-to-do anything, which excludes entertainment and distractions, concentrates on enhancing perception by only receiving incoming signals and observing their pathway through our bodies.

This deceptively simple, and oftentimes excruciatingly painful, practice is the beginning of self knowledge and what in Buddhist nomenclature is referred to as the Eightfold Path. Most important of these eight elements, from the point of view of a true Westerner, is *right action*. From the discipline of the senses, and of the mind, will start to become manifest a plethora of subtle signals the extent and credibility of which only the individual experiencing them can judge.

Presuppositions

One assumes that the person is able-bodied and retains a manner of freedom of movement and decision making. Being able to make use of time and at least a basic amount of resources in their own terms, that is, possessing a modicum of freedom, is a prerequisite to development. Otherwise, priority should bend entirely to the acquisition of the perceived level of liberty that will allow the leeway necessary for the individual to pursue their true desire (the discovery and development of which is a journey in its own right).

We also assume that the person undertaking these disciplines will have the predisposition to get results without the need to cling to a narrative or aesthetic path to the detriment of their individual reality and survival. Martyrs, heroes, saints, ideologues, idealists, psychos and other archetypes with suicidal tendencies are likely not suited to a path that will continually unveil that *what you believe is wrong* in a never-ending sequence that stops only when one realizes that *believing is a delusion*. Believing, of course, includes active non-belief. The *negating position* is as much a belief as the affirming one.

That is not to say that each person cannot have and indeed indulge in their preferences, to their pleasure and ecstasy. A person with a developing ear for their inner voice will gravitate to a highly individualized path, composed of things that call out to them. However, it is necessary that these things are not merely decorative; this, the heart will also tell, for when in balance and in contact with the rest of reality, something entirely superfluous will be perceived as nauseating. But, of course, these are the assumptions we make regarding the individuals approaching the practices and heuristics advocated herein.

Individual priorities

What an individual will choose to do, within the parameters described above, and on top of such a foundation, will differ with respect to interest and need. For instance, someone suffering from chronic physical discomfort in the joints, fatigue in the lower back, and so on, might be well advised to look first for solutions in that area. They might be called first to look into the Alexander Technique, which is all about posture correction towards what is natural for the human body in general and the proportions of the practitioner. From then on, a regimen of basic strength conditioning, mobility and displacement (i.e. walking, trekking, jogging, and so on) might be suitable. These are things we should all be partaking in, but we are calling to the reader's attention that investigating and developing them would be an enveloping first priority for those who recognize a sub-optimal use of their physical bodies.

Someone who has suffered throughout there life from a progressive worsening of the eyesight and eye health in general would be well advised to give eye care some attention. Mainstream resources as well as non-mainstream sources are worth looking into. In the latter classification, there is the Bates Method, which focuses on the idea that many people suffer from myopia or even astigmatism because of the *wrong use* of the eye. The idea here is that through correction of habits, the person can improve their eyesight as the health of the eye improves. The precise theory behind the Bates Method revolves revolves around the function of the muscular structure around the eye, and how our voluntary control can affect it. While decried by ophthalmologists since its inception as a fraud in the early twentieth century, it has never ceased having a hardcore following of people who claim to have found great relief by applying the Bates Method's exercises. It is worth noting that no appreciable niche industry has grown around the Bates Method, and its support and survival comes from advocates who read the original book and continued to share its principles.

People who struggle with sleep, chronic fatigue or illness, will find resources of all kinds directed at relaxation, a topic far more complex than one would imagine. This might start with a look into somatic therapy, the concern with nervous system health from the point of view of use. The underbelly of this movement has diversified quite a bit, but there is a backbone of medical and neuroscience support that has continued to validate and deepen the theory and practice of the related fields. Around the nuance and the admittedly useful exercises in the myriad approaches to somatic therapy, there is the notion that it all begins and ends with paying attention to sensations, and honoring them. The rabbit hole goes deep, and the surface is deceptively simple, which makes it even more confusing. However, somatic therapy is a bastion of natural health that we should look into. Some relevant names here include those of Peter Levine, Norman Doidge, and Stephen Porges.

The above are merely examples and simple guidelines. The idea is that each person will have to choose what they are most in need of developing or curing in themselves. Progression would mean that one of these practices becomes embedded, with sufficient knowledge to propel proper application, so that new areas of interest can be attended to efficiently. And while each person must follow an individual calling as to what is relevant and useful, there are a few obvious side quests that lead nowhere in particular and are a drain of time and resources. These include the obsession to learn many different languages without any concrete aim (are you going to write a book about it? Are you going to teach these languages? What are you going to DO with them?). Reading book after book on history, war, or magic and sorcery, amounts to the same, a kind of fetish. Equally useless is obsessive body building *for fun*, without a return flow in the form of money or usable status or health towards a *use*.

So many apparently respectable and useful things become obsessive distractions by the inability to be still and seriously consider what is *necessity* and what will actually facilitate an ascent. Most often, people stuck here have no access to guidance, or the value of guidance has been lost on them. It is as useless for a penniless man to be day-dreaming as it is for a well-off man to be working a day job "out of principle". Plan and act, acquire and use.

Mercurial and ethereal interests and their indulging are perfectly fine. But to those seeking dominion of their world, to break boundaries to their freedom and power, to enjoy life at a higher level, including the whims that give us pleasure moment to moment is of paramount importance. Yet this these must come within limits and context to your power and glory.

The Practice, not the Philosophy

Cynicism

One of the greater mental viruses of the modern age is the tendency for people to argue about principles without ever attempting the practice in whatever tradition or endeavor. Underneath it all lies cynicism. A Cynicism encoded into the very fabric of modern thought and the defining feeling of the scientist age, the information age, of overload, of totalitarian thought control. However, it did not start here.

The precursor to the Enlightenment tyranny was Christianity, with its dogma of oppression and conquest, of universality. Christianity, of course, in its institutional and cultural sense, with its morality. Not because rules and guidelines are entirely undesirable, but because those chosen by Christianity were meant to stifle, to bind the individual. The Enlightenment preached the contrary, but acted much the same. It was only an evolution of thought control. Each slave revolt needs a revision of the system of control. A new offering, a new allure, a new bait. Only Novalis caught on to the farce, and Goethe blocked his path for that.

So, today, the first question someone will ask you when invited or encouraged to do something is *why*. Even though, in theory, the scientific mind should only ask *how* and *why not*, because reason can only find out the means on the one hand, and disprove, on the other, but it cannot affirm the truth of a proposition regarding reality (by which we mean here, a *theory*) directly. People keep asking why, and supporting that why with prejudiced objections following a *but*. But everyone knows it doesn't work. But everyone knows it's bunk. But I don't think/know if it would work for me. But, but, but. That is, ideas before experience; often, laziness and apathy before a curious engagement with life, or at least the semblance of scientific interest.

Cynicism, in any case, is defeated easily. It is not a strong foundation for anything. If you hold a cynic attitude towards anything, you will have noticed that it takes energy to maintain that state. You need to remember *why* you are cynical. If you, in turn, asked *why not* be cynical, you would find plenty of reasons not to, and far superior to reasons for being cynical. The reasons for being cynical often amount to little more than resentment. Among the very concrete, down-to-earth reasons *why not* to be cynical are the fact that it causes constant stress and so forces your nervous system into an unsustainable stress (fight/flight/freeze) response that is, perhaps, the most common cause of premature aging, chronic fatigue, chronic illness, and much more.

Curiosity

One of the best ways to defeat cynicism is to engage in active, curious, playful exploration. Curiosity above all. We need curiosity. But curiosity of the experience. How does it feel, and what happens, when a certain experience takes place. We want to see things from the point of view of experience because experience is everything. No matter what you think or deduce or argue your mental models into later, it all comes from your individual experience of something. Reason comes later, and it is useful, it allows us to develop, to manipulate, so that we get what we want.

But reason without experience is empty. And to acquire experience, that is, to experience things (we want to use it as a verb as much as possible, because the word is a flux of events, not a landscape of abstractions), we must be curious. At least, if we want to experience things willingly and in a state of mind and conditions that we can control as much as possible (letting go of what we cannot). Otherwise, everything we experience will come from things that happen to us, that are imposed upon us.

The Use of Philosophy

Philosophy is defined as the love of knowledge. At least, in the mainstream. But this has been deformed, what with theology and the subsequent secular reaction to the infirmities of religious argument, and today it means some crude form of argumentation. Blame the interpreters of Socrates and Aristotle for this nonsense to begin with. Blame those who enthroned particularities of an ancient argument in context as the root and fountain of all philosophy. The calcification of ideas.

Love of knowledge, is it? If it is love of knowledge, then experience would be primary for the *philosopher*, and then reason, the power of argumentation, and logic, its tool, would be used to organize, to prod, to move forward and *experience* yet again, with more clarity. Philosophy cannot be an end. Experience must always be the end, because experience is life, experience is all we have, every moment, every single conscious moment. Philosophy in the favor of ideologies or religions is an empty exercise; it has to do with the building of vast edifices of abstractions which have nothing to do with *experience* (the only source of *realness*).

But, only experience is real.

All else is a model, a road map. Experience is the territory. Sure, Kant and physics tell us that what we perceive is only a fraction of the "real". But what of it? All this tells us is that we must deepen experience, because there is always more to discover, or that we can further course correct and perceive things more clearly, in more detail, or from a different angle. In any case, philosophy, on the contrary, can sometimes be but a map. And the map—is not the territory.

In all cases, the philosophy must serve the experience, and so should the science, the systematic application of reason. This is how we adhere to reality, by upholding the primacy of individual experience which is then compared, shared, validated or examined in comparison to that of others. Whether a reported experience fits a model or a theory should not be the disqualifying point, instead, it should go on file for possible evidence that disqualifies the theory. Once enough reported experiences from upstanding, credible individuals are turned in have accumulated, the notion should be validated that something *real* is happening for which the model cannot account. Back to the drawing board.

Why NOT Lucid Dreaming and Astral Projection?

Objections

"What's the point?" What's the point of anything? Lucid Dreaming and Astral Projection seem like insanely fun things to do, vastly superior to video games or digital virtual realities. They are also, reportedly, ways to get information quickly and at a distance. Yes, this is disputed even by people who are proficient in both, but the mere possibility of all of these things is stimulating to many people.

"But it takes so much time and effort." That depends. And besides, anything worth doing, and that you are going to derive great dividends from, is likely to take time and effort. This objection will only deter the kind of person who will not work for anything in their life for more than two seconds.

"Why would I *believe* these things are even real." Well, for one, Lucid Dreaming has been proven in a laboratory setting and is considered a factual experience since at least the late 70s. In the case of the Out-of-Body Experience (aka Astral Projection), it has been reported for thousands of years by scores of people. Just in the last one hundred and fifty years there have been compilations of these experiences put together by living credible people, gathering such accounts from other living credible people. You could look into the work of Robert Crookall for these references.

Implications

Lucid Dreaming and Astral Projections are frameworks for disembodied experiences. In essence all dreaming is an Out-of-Body Experience (OBE) because you are not acting in an environment with your physical body. This is why Michael Raduga has opted for calling all conscious disembodied states *the phase*. The only downside to Raduga's approach, and it is an understandable downside, is that his research subscribes to the materialist notion. It appears that he believes that all experience and consciousness arises from the brain, or the nervous system, at any rate.

Wider implications, unfettered by materialist assumptions, should be obvious. We are not just conventionally considered material bodies, and our consciousness can exist separate from the body. Now, while many people at this point go wild with assumptions, this does not prove immortality not even the fact that we can exist without the body. Unfortunately many smart people jump wagon here and go full spiritualist in one go.

While there are indications that some people's consciousness have survived bodily death, we do not know if this is an immortality situation, or of it is just a matter of gradually fading into oblivion. The only thing Lucid Dreaming proves is that we can consciously take control of our dreams. The only thing OBEs prove is that we can experience a facet of consciousness in a state that appears to us, for all practical purposes, to take place outside of the body.

Lucid Dreaming is proven "objectively", that is validated even for people who report never having had this experience.

Astral Projection is only validated between people who have had this experience.

From the practical point of view, of attaining any of these experiences, Raduga's perspective is useful. Instead of thinking you must transcend into another plane, you simply acknowledge the fact that every night you dream, and every time you dream you have the possibility of becoming aware that you are dreaming, i.e. to become lucid. In that state, you have the chance of going into a full-blown astral projection. According to Raduga, the difference between the dream, the lucid dream and the astral projection is a matter of degree. The Phase, as he calls it, is this brain-produced experience. Raduga is very wise in approaching the experience this way, purposefully avoiding any philosophical discussions, ducking arguments, tying the very mystical experience of astral projection to an already objectively proven phenomenon in lucid dreaming. This way, he becomes eligible for public funding, and is more accessible for mainstream consideration.

For the individual practitioner, taking what works from Raduga and then discovering how these alternate realities work is the most productive. The idea that it is all connected, for one, can facilitate success. But it is the implication which we must manage. The implications must remain open-ended until experience connects certain dots. And even then, conclusions must never supersede experience.

Remote Viewing for Stabilizing the Artist's State of Flow

The idea of remote viewing as a martial art was brought to our attention by Joseph McMoneagle as he draws parallels between the remote viewing need to reach a level of mental stability and openness akin to that found in Zen practice and the spirit of Japanese martial arts. While in the first chapter of his book, *Remote Viewing Secrets: A Handbook*, MacMoneagle proceeds to install subliminal linguistic directives into the reader for the purpose of setting mental safeguards preventing rogue behavior as much as possible, he also communicates useful pointers for the practice of remote viewing which could have an application to progress and mastery of any activity. Ideas such as not aiming for perfection but for the mind-quieted state of flow that brings through a constant stream of perceptions, have a somewhat similar echo in the rules for learning that Feldenkrais developed as a consequence of his Judo training.

One of the most salient features of remote viewing is that you should put down exactly what you perceive and nothing—we repeat— *nothing* else. The state of mind required is that of total presence, something we experience when in a duel, a physical altercation, whether in tournament or outside, but also during the act of sexual intercourse—if properly approached. These acts consume our minds entirely, and there is a magic released therein that comes from the fact that we are able to engross ourselves so deeply and with all our senses that we exist nowhere else at any other point in time. At least, that is how it feels. It is a state of flow, or what some would rather term *the zone*.

This state is also sought by artists and scientists alike. A state in which ideas, schemata, pictures, all come in completed form, all outside the step-wise, cumbersome ways of reason. In other words, the highway of inspiration. Conventionally, the highest form of artists know that when inspiration hits, they must take advantage of this moment. So do scientists. The cleverest among them will have developed an "ear", so to speak, of what state of mind personally brings about such state of flow, such inspiration that is an openness to intuition, to messages in completed form, perhaps even to a kind of Platonic world of forms extant somewhere beyond the veil.

Remote viewing training aims at making the practitioner able to enter this state at will, on demand. The protocols aimed at directing consciousness to take advantage of this state do so with the specific and explicit aim of gathering technical sensory information. Nevertheless, it is admitted by military professionals such as Ed Dames that the controlled remote viewing protocol can be used to obtain more speculative type of answers concerning decisions or the existence of a certain target object. This tells us there could also be a way of adapting controlled remote viewing protocols to facilitate artistic flow.

Where does imagination enter, you might ask. Herein lies the confusion, while there is much imagination in art, be it literature, music, sculpture, poetry, or anything else, all of the best artists, as well as the best appreciators of art, will concur that the best art does not come from mere imagination. Its is admitted among whispers that the greatest art comes from "elsewhere", behind the seat of the mind, from a greater awareness, a greater consciousness of which the regular individual mind is but a drop, a tendril among trillions.

The essential elements of the remote viewing protocol, abstracted in order to produce a working model applicable to the artistic process, are three. The first is veiling or avoiding attempts to prematurely define the final result as much as possible. The second is being able to rhythmically record flash-impressions coming as pulses into awareness before the process of imaginative construction gets started. The third is having a framework of vessels into which the aforementioned impressions will be recorded; that is, a systematic way of giving form to the energy, perhaps in the form of archetypes.

In literature in particular, many are the character and plot building frameworks that seek to give would-be writers a guide to clear expositions. Oftentimes, these result in weak, stale products which, even if successful, are recognized as artistic failures and empty caricatures but more sensitive demanding personalities. The problem, it would seem, is that the workers of literature more prone to using prepared character and plot frameworks are not the kind that connect well with higher artistic principles. On the other hand, more accomplished, sensitive artists, readily see in frameworks a tying of their hands, a limiting of their creativity. The latter confuse creativity with inspiration, the real source of breakthrough original works of art. Not even Heidegger can convince us otherwise. The ground of being demands to be listened to, while all the noise around, all the appearing, and the will to appear, interrupts communication, distorts the message.

If all the strangeness and intensity of the spirit of Stravinsky's Rite of Spring could be funneled into potent vessels with shapes like those dreamed up by Giger, and mounted on a progressive sequence of scenes each commanding more interest and tension than the one before, and yet each a standalone aesthetic pleasure, you would have a magnetic work of towering genius.

But to make a system and method of training that allows the artist to summon such forces to his aid, a conscious adherence to protocol, and at the same time a relinquishing of personal control, would have to occur. The creation of an unusual system of vessels arranged for plot and depth, defined in their contours but not their total flavor, in their order and relations, but not their actions. And then a wild recording of chaos, punctuated by pauses to halt and divert the plot-building impulses of the mind; a record of these chaotic outbursts, preferably in states violent and sensual, would be summoned up by quick prompts to be "probed into" without thinking and followed up by spasmodic event-recording.

The possibilities are many, the road more demanding than before, yet the end also more promising for the adventurous artist.

Journal—*Intensely*

Journal your daily events, the stages of your life, your dreams, what did not happen but could have happened, summon the ghosts of the past and the future, visit alternate timelines, gain wisdom from the multiverse. This, and much more, is why you should journal—*intensely*.

The Intense Journal Method was created by the Jewish psychiatrist Ira Progoff. It stems from Jungian notions, principally, that there exist, somewhere in consciousness, forms called archetypes, living forms representing ideas and concepts, and with which one can interact as one would with a sentient being. The approach would perfectly blend in within a therapeutic setting, while it would not be alien to the occult altogether.

Progoff's main idea is that one journal would contain different section in which you would attend to different levels and perspectives of your mind, understanding by putting it all together into one work that your experience is all united with yourself as a nexus. On different sections of the journal you would be exploring hard facts without embellishments, while on others you would explore events that never happened but could have.

Recording dreams, something that is also included in the Intense Journal Method, has been singled out as the most straightforward and useful way for beginners to start lucid dreaming. Although this does not seem to have been Progoff's main motivation for including a dream log in the method, it is a welcome added benefit. Lucidity tends not to arrive by accident.

Independently of whether it comes through the act of logging your dream experiences, getting into the habit of questioning whether you are in a dream throughout the day, or looking at your hands periodically (yes, this actually works), the lucid experience comes from a conscious decision to enhance awareness of direct experience. What direct experience means here is detailed attention to sensory input while acting, to the exclusion of building constructs, getting carried away by emotions or lost in thoughts. It is an exercise that can be practiced while awake, making it a habit for yourself to do this at all time. If the effort is serious, this will quickly result in a spillover into your dreaming experience.

Journaling will also help you revise your daily habits. Humans have a legendary ability to tell themselves stories about what they are doing, what they want, and where they want to go. One of the things that will happen when you start logging your days is that leaks and habits that do not match your *ideas* of what you are doing with your life are quickly exposed. The divergence between what you believe you desire and the actions you are taking on the daily appear now as a very noticeable rift. You can then either look away and try to ignore it or you revise that relationship. That is, it is not always a matter of correcting the course of your actions to meet your stated desires. Very often, what is really happening is that what you tell yourself you want comes from the outside, from constructs, or from an overactive imagination, or a logical mind bouncing down a staircase of deductive possibilities.

The revising of a life, defining the important milestones along it, and revisiting the crucial feelings and possibilities that existed from one era to another, has been a process that psychologists and psychiatrists of different stripes have acknowledged as useful and as usually having a great impact. The Intensive Journal Method also has a space for doing so. Besides the more obvious excavation of old problematic feelings that were in the past bottled up and started causing problems, we can see how revising the distant past ties in with the daily log. Your actions and decisions are laid out before you so that you start to gain clarity of why you are where you are, and clues arise as to why there has been any confusion to begin with.

Moreover, as the different logs in the journal start to fill out, and more thought experiments and Jungian explorations start to take place, the instructions for the Intensive Journal will start to guide you into making connections from one area of the journal into another. When that happens, you will start to weave a braid with the levels of consciousness and areas of life experience, so that the boundaries between these which were initially of much use in pin-pointing aspects of an experience, become blurred, and the perception of life starts to arise as the interlinked mass of events and processes that it is. At this point, it is not just that one becomes aware of the river and the different elements in it, nor that one allows the flow to take precedence, but a certain mastery of several currents starts to become possible. This can only be discovered individually. The present is an invitation.

Walking the Tightrope

A false dichotomy

Wellness and devotion, self-care and self-discipline, accomplishment and satisfaction; we are told we must choose between these, that one ingrains us here on earth, and on the walls of the ethereal halls of the gods, while the other is a waste of our existence by way of indulgence. In occult parlance, the proposition that discipline defined by the divine is the only way, and that individual indulgence is inadequate, constitutes the beginning of the bifurcation of the path of esoteric attainment into the Left and Right Hand paths. The interested reader can look further into the abundant extant literature on this division.

When we look closely at this matter, without prejudice or partisanship, we can understand that both sides have a point. On the one hand, there are habits and lifestyles that lead to self-destruction, to blindness, and to constant suffering. On the other, it would not make sense to say no to the pleasures of existence for the sake of an invisible, a promised, salvation in a future or a reality we cannot even grasp.

From there, more becomes obvious. First, that there must exist a middle path neither to one extreme nor the other. Second, that this middle path should address and satisfy the concerns the more it is perfected. Beyond the immediately evident, divergences in opinions and in preference highlight the need for each person's path to be tailored to themselves as a unique vector mapped across multiple higher dimensions. How and what these are can be best left to individual exploration and an eventual convergence of related experience.

Absolute self-interest

From our point of view, the perfected path that unites the proper, the constructive, the ennobling, with the enjoyment of pleasure, the satisfaction of thirst for knowledge and experience, lies in absolute self-interest. Note that we do not mean selfishness or egoism in the conventional uses of these words. The words hide more than it seems, and they point to a demanding process whereby self-satisfaction leads not to careless indulgence but to a process whereby the deepest desires of a person are brought to the surface.

We humans have been referred to as matrices. There is the greater matrix within which we all interact, and within which also greater symbols and possibilities float and resonate with or repel each other. But the individual matrix of the human encasing has to do with whatever you bring as a conscious observer, the body into which you were set (the ancients would have thought this determines *destiny* and *fate*, depending on calibration), and the degree of awareness (i.e. the degree to which you are awake and aware that you are an observer of experience at the very core).

In following this model of the interrelations between elements of reality being one large matrix comprised of an ocean and hierarchy of matrices within matrices, outside influences, the trends, the important symbols that affect and influence our lives, lie somewhere close to us, at least in magnitude and significance. So it becomes evident that not all that you desire, not all that you think and feel, belongs necessarily to you. Thoughts and feelings are signals. They are not good or bad, and they may have different sources. It is no wonder why the central practice of meditation, and to some extent prayer, have to do with increasing an awareness with a connection to existence while allowing these signals to pass by unheeded. As we progress our ability to differentiate the source of the signals improves. A distinct path to a deeper source within and beyond ourselves becomes clearer.

Absolute self-interest, our proposed concept, leads to a doubling down, a concentrating, in the awareness of the boundaries of the individual, the extent of their interests in terms of mental magnetism (a term freely use, without conscious relation to the New Thought movement), and the development of what the individual is geared to by virtue of the body and time given to them.

The first filter: Know thyself

To know thyself is a very old adage. A story is told that you can take the time to look into. Philosophical discussions around it abound. The core of the matter is that to arrive at self-knowledge sounds simple, because the work is straightforward, but it is nevertheless hard. You may be reminded that you know what you must do, but you also realize it is not easy to do. That is not to say that the actions you are called to take are necessarily hard, but rather the decision to willingly endure the friction to go against the inertia of your past actions, including possible social fallout and the rejection or setting aside of mores and morals you had till then upheld as true.

Practitioners of Tao and Zen are well-aware of the dictum, *sleep when tired, eat when hungry*. Not a state, but a process. Now, how does this tie in with knowing oneself? Let's take a closer look.

Religious movements will seek refuge in prophets, in leaders who *we must trust* are in contact with the divine. All while acknowledging that God, the divine, the greater or deeper Self, however one wants to approach the phenomenon, exist in constant, permanent, connection with each of us. All that keeps you from that direct connection and instead paying attention to someone else about what you should or should not do is fear, and the lack of dedication that can lead you to the establishment and strengthening of that direct link to the point where no intermediaries are necessary.

It is very possible that the deceptively simple approach of the Oriental tradition contained within the phrase *sleep when tired, eat when hungry* contains the basic practice to *follow your impulse* in the deepest sense. To learn to really listen to the pains and aches, the needs, the joys, and warnings, and so on, that come through with your body. Whatever we are, ultimately, irrespective of modes presented to us by one or other tradition, the fact of the matter is that we process all incoming signals in the form of sensations, either directly in the body or similar translations into feelings and intuitions in the nervous system. Whether the perception of these signals originate in the physical body or elsewhere is beside the point. The point is to listen closely, and eventually achieve a more nuanced differentiation of their nature and origin.

The art of distinguishing the different impulses and learning to *choose for oneself* could fill tomes (a work that we might undertake, given time, but the time is too early for a work of such metaphysical magnitude), yet the practice consists almost solely of paying attention and remaining aware of what goes on. Pleasure and pain will come and go, and what we feel most compelled to choose constitutes desire. The choice that comes from the unwavering place no matter the mood nor preference of the day qualifies as an authentic desire. We say this to distinguish desire from caprice. Desire arises from magnetism, and when one speaks or writes too much about it, the text rapidly devolves into vagaries, into a pastiche of sophistries. It is therefore imperative that the interested party make of the affair a practice, a habit, and that he incorporates it into daily life, so that from the notion's seed a stem and leaves grow green, and, finally, that a flower therefrom blossom.

The second filter: Do what works

Desire (discovered, cultivated, allowed to grow) serves as a compass. We might descend too deep into speculation if unguarded, but let us venture to say that if there are indeed physical and nonphysical aspects to us, desire might come from the physical matrix and also from some ulterior place, connected to a preternatural origin. Why even go into this territory unaided by scores of theological artillery or some kind of authority to back it up? Firstly, and aside from the reason that is pertinent here, to the authentically thinking person, argument and authority matter very little. A satanist would even say they matter less than nothing. Secondly, a careful self-examination can very easily yield plausible explanations as to why one holds one desire or another. Quite often, asking oneself out loud or writing the question down with the intent of getting an answer is enough to trigger a first response. To keep digging, one keeps asking, intelligently, why, for what purpose, and so on, and comparing the answers that come to mind with the feelings that arise in parallel. Self-honesty will reveal that the answers have been known all along. Certain things are liked, indulged in, sought, simply because friends, environment, or perhaps even the alignment of the stars (ask Ptolemy) guided us there. If we stop and *observe* and allow the sensations that come with the perception of said influences move through us, as one would with pain and emotion (ask Shinzen Young), they are washed away, by the force and current of the same waves that brought them to our doorstep. Then there remains the thinnest of threads, the yearnings which have no visible link to your living experiences, nor to the circumstances of your upbringings. The mark upon these will be twofold. First will be the aforementioned lack of a conscious link to anything palpable in your mortal life. Second will be the consistency inherent in them, the sense of permanency, revealed by the fact that as you hold still, they, too, shall hold still *with you.*

What will work in the long run for the individual without doing violence to the Self (and to the body), will likely have something to do with these desires with preternatural links. But what will work also has two aspects. The first is, as mentioned, determined by the motivating desire's relation to the Self, the Lord, the Observer. The second concerns method and circumstance to implement the road of action once the aim has been determined. This is the other side of the coin. With one hand you reach deep into yourself and you let the world move around. With the other, you feel out the terrain, for the terrain is all-important here, and the route taken must adapt to it. The search for, the building of, the seeking of a desired state, would be best served, for your own sake, by the most efficient means.

Doing what works, as described above, has levels to it, and levels that are deeply personal, defined by individuality. How they are attended to, organized, promoted or demoted, can only be discovered through the first step, knowing yourself. The process might not end, but it does not mean that further and further stability and strength are not gained. They are, if one succeeds, which is a matter of putting in the work. The greatest distractions to realizing the core work are caprices and a false sense of belonging to a greater whole wherein individuality is lost, for the sake of a dream given, curated, and dictated for a purpose alien to yourself. So, choose, or a choice will be made for you. And then, again, and so on.

Doing what works works along an axis sustained by *what works for you* and *what works for the environment*. You cannot disregard either of them and expect for things to go smoothly. Things will go the smoothest when you *pay attention* and develop *acuity*, the capacity to perceive states and changes in states, and the talent to adapt to them, switching gears until a variation of approach clicks.

Some things are, nevertheless, unavoidable and are part of the nature of reality. The work must be put it. It does not mean it needs to be hard. Difficulty as a measure of the worthiness or value of an effort is a red herring. But to learn, to allow for adaptations in neurology and other physiology to take place, repetition, reinforcement and consistency in general must be in place. So much, we all know.

The only measure of worthiness, at the end of the day, remains in the question: *Does It Work?*

All else is hubris.

"It don't matter what you believe"

Once direct experiencing of your senses becomes primary, it becomes quite clear that thoughts and emotions are circumstantial. Beliefs and convictions fall by the wayside. The focus upon what is happening around you, what your eyes perceive, your ears hear, and the relationships between input and output become clearer and clearer, the models political, ideological, religious, cosmological, and so on, for the world, that a person might have are revealed as spurious, as irrelevant.

To the average person walking in the street, whether the Earth is flat, round, spherical, cubic, pyramidal or tetrahedral, has no relevance at all. What matters to you as you walk out the door, look up at the sky, see the curvature of the dome above, enjoy the play of colors in the firmament with the sun setting into the distance, many miles away into the horizon, is that you are experiencing these things, as you see them, this very moment. The models for the shape of the planet do not change the world around you, just as the different psychological models for human mind do not change your experience as a person after you have learned to focus on direct observation.

Abraham Maslow came up with the pyramid of needs. Is it accurate? Where did he get this? How did he gather this data? There is common sense in the thing, but is it universal? Does it apply in every case? More importantly, would you forget to be hungry, to want a mate, to seek out respect and status, if you had never seen Maslow's model of human needs painted on a screen or a book? It is doubtful.

The facts and forces will accumulate, and reality will make you notice it exists. It will do so in no uncertain terms. Tread carefully, we must. That does not mean reality does not evolve, that the rules do not change. Nor that the past may not change. Large scale random number generator experiments in the area of parapsychology have yielded results that indicate that collective willpower can bend probabilistic expectations towards the unlikely. And yet, there is a persistence, a loyalty to what has actually happened, that no mass deception campaign can succeed in changing the past into a fairy tale unless most of the people who knew it to be false are killed off.

What you believe, will only add layers to what you can see, hear and touch. Sometimes, these things are useful. Most of the time, they lead you into patterns of thoughts designed to direct you in accordance with a greater will. So, the question we have to ask ourselves remains, master or slave. *What will ye?*

Where beliefs matter

Belief matters as a trigger for action. Belief, for the savvy practitioner, should never be confused with reality. It should be, nevertheless, included as a tool among many. The problem of the majority is to be consumed by belief, duped by belief. Belief constructs a system of assumptions, honing your mind into certain lines of thought and so of possible action. Belief will also foster certain desires to the exclusion of others. It acts as a filter between possible events surrounding you and the experiences that become plausible for you.

We do not mean here to say that mere superficial belief is going to change reality. A superficial belief is usually the will to disbelieve something else; that is, the person *trying* to belief, or pretending to believe something is only running away from something else. The art of believing and disbelieving at will requires a very clear cognizance of the nature of belief in relation to reality.

The application of belief for its best effect, however, can be a bit tricky. Too much of it and it can cloud your judgment, lead you astray, and leave you in a fairyland of your own making. That is precisely the case with most people that we could say fall in the mind-controlled category. They share an illusion, or a delusion, and they are completely unaware of it. But the best use of belief is the conscious use of an illusion that enhances focus, that filters out the unnecessary, and makes things *click* for us. Most important here is also that last bit: *for us.*

Perform Trials, then Confirm or Reject

Instead of belief (or its corresponding opposite force, *disbelief*), we want to approach our subject and our actions with as clean a mind as possible, using our power to reason in the most scientific way possible, rather than to spin stories that can then be layered over what is happening.

While belief has its uses, if we are always aware that we are simply putting on a suit when using it, we are really just adhering to a model rather than developing a belief (or a "blind belief", as people commonly say). To use this terminology is more clear. We do not believe in things, we simply use a model that so far works well for our purposes. If the model yields results, then we have a functional tool. Otherwise, it is not the model we need.

Trusting Sensations

Poetry, abstract and tangible

One of the lessons W.B. Yeats imparted to Ezra Pound was that abstractions muddied communication, they introduced barriers to communication. Reportedly, the older poet told the younger one to look through his poems and see how many abstractions he could find. And it seems he found many such abstractions in his text, to his own surprise. As he moved forward, Pound sought to transform his expression into more something more graspable, with objects and motions at the very center of his work.

While Pound later stirred into a mystic obscurantism and rhythmic experimentation, it is quite obvious that the dictum of avoiding abstraction was preserved. Understand or not, we can recognize the symbols, the agents, the scenes, and the actions depicted line after line in his poetry. And even when we do not recognize a name or title, nor even the context, we know that what stands before us is a symbol, a person, or an agent—a personality, at any rate.

When we pay attention to what happens inside ourselves as we shift a conversation from descriptive actions to abstractions, we will become aware of a sort of disconnection, as if we are no longer, not entirely, *here*. The eyes become glazed, they stare nowhere. The typical look of the mystic or the dreamer is that of someone who has left the present, shared reality. The disconnection occurs with the body itself and in great part with other people around them. This type of person is not misunderstood or sundered socially because they or their ideas are strange or special, in the sense of them being hard to come by. They are simply harder to understand for most people because of how they are expressed. If one cared to pay attention, the highest philosophical ideas, if they make any sense at all, can be found all over the artistic production of the human mind. More importantly, you will come across these ideas in the events of daily life.

Plato and the World of Forms

Let us consider for a moment that abstraction comes as a mistrust of the senses. We will not argue that abstraction begun with Christianity, for we can find abstract thought before. Now, some have said point blank that abstracting itself lead to the downfall of humanity, much like Gibbon wrote Christianity had been the downfall of the Roman Empire. Many agreed with him. We also know that Christians and Muslims praise Aristotle and Plato, coming very close to naming them *honorary* members of their religions. What these two shared with the aforementioned religions was that impulse to abstraction.

May we come in Plato's defense and point out that his depictions of discussions of abstractions were couched in dialogues, and that said dialogues in the mouth of Socrates and his differing companions tended to resort to concrete examples. Thus, happiness was never left as an abstraction, but was always brought down to earth. We can, in fact, see Socrates as the hero who always makes concrete the abstract. Plato makes sure we are always coming back to particulars, to actions. Even as there is a *world of forms* above ours, for which his ideas are mainly known, it is not so much the imaginary *world of abstractions* of modern scholarship, as it is, possibly, something more akin to the *astral world* of modern occultism.

The impulse to act, the signal to respond, neuroscience experiments have shown, comes before the conscious mind is aware of that the action is taking place. The reasoning mind organizes, makes plans, abstracts and feeds this back. It rationalizes decisions. The act itself, the action, comes from something either *behind* it or *above* it.

Consciously, we become aware of what we sense, in the actions that are taking place, in the inputs we receive from the outside, and in the impulses that come deep from within us. And so it would appear that to know and control more, we must be very careful with abstraction and rationalization. As with many other mental traps, they can be useful tools and allies, as well as terrible traps and traitors.

Ownership and Value, An Example of the Traps of Abstraction

Abstractions can be helpful in organizing and moving things around inside our heads, but if we are seeking to extend our capacity in the world, to do, to experience, and so on, they cannot supersede our sensations. Very often, abstractions are used to hoodwink, to divert, and they are prominently recognized as part of the arsenal of sorcery (*this is not a poetic exaggeration or embellishment*). While we do not endorse ideologies of any kind, we do understand that our society has embraced abstract concepts to the point where the useful verges on abusive.

One such abstract concept, ownership, was useful as long as it concerned the *respect* afforded an individual as to his claim to be the main user of an object. It is entirely based on an invented rule so that there can be an understanding between two individuals. In truth, ownership does not exist. Thinking it does is being deluded. Such delusion is what lies at the root of many individuals feeling surprised, or even "appalled", when people with greater power and absolutely no respect for them see it fit to transgress the boundaries of said ownership. Your things may be destroyed, taken away, and so on, and short of retribution by way of the law or your own hands, there is no stopping it. The concept of ownership will not stop it.

The *agreement* of ownership, as any other social abstraction, can only exist as a *compromise* between individuals. It is a compromise towards peace. If no such peace is desired, and if no respect is forthcoming, you can be sure abstractions will not come to your aid.

The delusion of ownership, to continue with this particular example, allows for even more covert means of subversion. Imagine you are told that, in exchange for your work and effort you will be given tokens, or "credits". Imagine then, that these tokens or credits do not have a fixed value, but that they fluctuate. In fact, as a general rule, they will automatically and indefinitely become less and less valuable as time goes by. This, of course, will not happen on its own. The value that you have acquired did not just disappear. The effect of your actions did not simply fizzle out. Energy does not disappear. The value and recompense of your actions continues moving in effect, along and across people and processes. You, however, will only receive a one-time, depreciating token, the value of which is a caprice, in exchange for the potentially infinite benefit you give to others. The tokens are a useful con, but a con nonetheless. The abstraction at the root of the great fraud is the concept of *value*.

The argument here is not a Marxist one. Marx's single pony trick revolves around "correctly" calculating value and arguing in favor of a more "just" system. What we are pointing out here, in contrast, is that the ground upon which all such arguments exist is an artifice.

The Power in the Senses

Remote viewing in particular was designed with the explicit purpose of eliminating the distracting effects of abstraction, rationalization and identification from the process of direct perception. The whole purpose of the systematic protocols of remote viewing have to do with getting rid of the deductions and associations, of the wistful creativity, and to simply *perceive what is*.

The degree to which importance is laid on this aspect is so great that in the old days, reportedly, remote viewers in training were suggested to study and practice the drawing exercises in Betty Edward's book *Drawing on the Right Side of the Brain*. Said exercises emphasize creating in oneself the habit of only capturing the information that is brought to our eyes by the light, and nothing else. Usually, we pass over things, identifying and categorizing them. We see a lamp or a chair, and what we tend to consciously remember and picture is an archetypal lamp or chair. What we see, however is an arrangement of shadows upon a screen of light that comes to the retina of the eye. We *touch the world* with our eyes.

Entering the *phase*, as Michael Raduga calls lucid dreaming and the out-of-body experience, is all about a *deepening of physical sensations*. This flies in the face of most "astral" rhetoric of the New Age and "occult" variety. Raduga, however, a single-minded beast of tremendous willpower turned educator and scientist, cares only for effective procedures divested of veiling rhetoric.

Phasing procedures, the protocols taught by Michael Raduga, hitherto known as "awakening in dreams", "projecting into the astral", "going into a hypnagogic state of mind", and so on, consist from beginning to end in utilizing different techniques that bring to increasing focus and activation the function of one or another physical sense while remaining physically still. Imagining, visualizing, is only used as a secondary psychic driving technique, so as to predispose the mind towards a definite result. All is included for merely functional uses directed at producing said result. Nevertheless, at the forefront of all is to sink into the sensations, to test sensations, to *enhance* sensations, to the point you can hear, touch, smell, move, and so on more and more independently of the situation or condition in which the physical body is.

Modern Art and Abstraction

The signature of all modern art is its tendency to abstract, to go from actuals to conceptuals, to subvert perception of aesthetic through argument, to impose the mind upon the senses, and then to claim that such inversion is the authentic, the natural. The argument can also take the form of an entire dismissal of the natural. They do so by claiming that the idea of something being natural or unnatural is entirely conceptual. Because in effect, this is true, here is where a muddying of the waters of the mind takes place.

We exist as total beings with sets of faculties, abilities, and so on, that allow us to sense the world, organize it, distinguish patterns. Our internal chemistry and electric patterns react, redefining the shape of texture and organ, bone and muscle, rallying the thunderstorm roaring in the brain into battles. The real is the whole of this apparent chaos (which it is not). We exist as individuals because there is pattern, because personality and individuality arise, and because we sense, as a species and then as a subset of that, as individuals.

The great deception, the great enslavement, consists in this: making us forget about the sensations, of the world, of the internal movements of the body, and their extensions, as primary. Instead, we are given images, longings outside of ourselves. This is not an argument against ego or desire. On the contrary, the root and fountain of these lies within, through the senses.

Just Enough

One of the traps of being oriented towards self-education and of having great intellectual curiosity for things is to get bogged down in a swamp of theory and accounts for far longer than is necessary. While each new endeavor requires a manner of guidance, the basic foundational skills of almost any discipline, need only a straightforward instruction. The rest is consistent practice.

There is something else to know, another book to read, another author to consult, a different way of doing things. You could go on indefinitely, discovering new patterns and paradigms. Potentially, there are as many ways of projecting as conscious beings in the world, in addition to the permutations introduced by collaboration and interaction, and the variations thereof. But we, as individuals, can either remain the spectators of the show, or we can become participants. Furthermore, the degree to which we become the sole captains, decision makers, of our every action, stylistic choice and knowers of our desires, is the degree to which we become the main actors within our individual perceptions.

What we are advocating is cutting, simply cutting. The idea, as received here, comes from Miyamoto Musashi, the famous Japanese duelist. Infamous on the arena, the warrior emphasized practicality and trusting the senses. He argued for a state of emptiness. While we are not experts in Eastern philosophy, we reserve the right to expound our interpretations of these words through our experience through life, through effort. Void, in its most functional aspect, has simply to do to stop fantasizing and over-elaborating, over-extending. Some would say that you "become one" with your surroundings. Others, closer to home, would say you are "extending your senses". As a rule, we would rather say you are *paying attention* to what is going on. And this, to an uncommonly experienced degree that allows you to move and react with the ever-changing chain of cause and effect, even before it unfolds.

The point of consumption, if one is to take control of one's world, is to enable, to feed, to grow stronger, to assimilate, to become more lethal, to take more heads, shrinking them and having the spirits within them serve us. Each person shall take these words as they will, in accordance with their predisposition and prejudice, or, hopefully, lack thereof.

Hundreds if not thousands of fatalists and decadents can argue. For it is their right to indulge for no reason at all. Their birthright to wallow in apathy and decide it is not for them to accept the animal inside, but only feed it palliatives to dampen the pain of the hungry wound. They say they indulge the wound, befriend the beast, and you will forgive them for they know not what they say, and certainly not what they do.

But you, what will you do?

Hereby do we incite all in our train, or within sight of it, to indulge in creation, referencing just enough, consuming to strengthen, and to produce non-stop. Journals, drawings, manifestos, methods, businesses, whatever it is. For they are a manifestation of your power and glory. Whoever tries to convince us that all is lost, that we can do nothing, because we are nothing, has something to gain from our consumption of their words, their products, and in some way or other, you become food for them. We reject such a path. We take just enough for our benefit, to enhance our knowledge, and so our power. And we rise.

enough for our benefit, to enhance our knowledge, and so our power. And we rise.

World Domination

Push everything away, and allow your desire alone to remain. This is the road we have increasingly taken on our journey of accomplishment. As far as we can see, it works for everything. It is also a tricky thing.

When you follow every whim, chances are you are being diverted into giving away your time, money, energy, and so on, to something that gives you nothing back, or just a temporary respite from your suffering. You suffer because you want more life, more power, more choice, more of your desires laid on your lap.

When we underline remote viewing and the out-of-body experience as expedient roads to a form of power over your life, we did so under the pretense of these things opening unknown doors, doors that reveal more of what you want and give you more choices, more possibilities. We also know that some will resonate with the prospect and the method, and others will not. This is as expected and is for the best, for it is in line with following desire. You should do this and all other things because it is what you desire, one way or another.

Follow this line of thinking, examine the why of every decision, and you will find hidden desires under things you consciously reject or detest about your life. The slave loves being a slave, the subdued is addicted to hating and desires to be told what to do and given sustenance in the mouth.

Subliminal Self-Subversion

Anton LaVey, in one of his many essays, later collected shortly before or after his death, argued in favor of acquiring total control of subliminal influence over oneself. A tantalizing proposition, the precise method he gave was to create all sensory inputs you would customarily consume. These included all the forms of art in which you would indulge, as well as an extreme personalization of your living surroundings. Furthermore, LaVey suggested we record psychic driving tapes (read as self-hypnotizing, "self-help" tapes, and so on, but aesthetically and purpose tailored to ourselves), and voodoo-like dolls and other paraphernalia extremely customized to your desires and worldly designs.

We need not operate exactly as the founder of the Church of Satan intended. His suggestion is, in fact, to act in whatever matter most pleases you and expresses your personality.

Now, imagine being free enough, in mind and intention, to create the music you would rather listen, write the novels and research you would see carried out, living in a house where every corner, symbol displayed, and so on, has a meaning and an effect that is in line with your aim, either through pleasure or displeasure (for both can be harnessed to your benefit).

Increasingly, the scenario becomes akin to the ill-named Chaos Magick of Peter J. Carroll et al. As the artist deepens in his personalization of the total experience of life under self-influence, even the symbols he uses, the divinities he worships, arise from a cosmos entirely of his own making. A blind Ouroboros, self-consuming and self-directed. It is said that somehow, sometime, if the individual survives the onslaught brought about by their own deluge, the cyclonic power of the process starts to spill over into the worlds (perception-domains) of other conscious entities (including that of other humans).

Lawlessness and the Outlaw

Riding the incessant waves of the Will, clashing rhythmically and cyclically against the rocky coastline of our physical body, we discover the inner life of the outlaw. The only law turns out to be the attainment of our desires, their full-fledged and unrestrained indulgence. The only measure of worthiness and success is how much the both the road and the never-ending process pleases us. The moment it ceases to do so, you have gone wrong.

Think not in terms of pigeonholed philosophical categories. Think in terms of functions, of remaking and retaking mechanistic contraptions to make something of your own. We do not advocate a motley approach, wherein you end up with a patchwork of mismatched symbols and semi-truths. What we mean is that where you find truth that *serves your budding desire*, take it. Take it as it suits you, take it out of context, as long as it works in your context. Make it yours. For the outlaw, it is their own law that matters alone.

Hence the bare-bones methods and approaches suggested by us. That they may serve all of the highly individual readers approaching our publications. Because we do not preach a doctrine, reserving the right to display our desire, and sharing what works.

In the end, it is quite simple. Stop and listen. Take control. Chain and master whatever is holding you back, and make it your steed to ride upon.

For the mystery of lawlessness is
already at work, but only until the
one who now restrains it is removed.

Did you love *Kosmokrator*? Then you should read *Prohibition*[1]
by D.A.R.G.!

[2]

A genetically and psychologically engineered man recounts the story of his transformations, his flight for freedom and the untimely demise of more than one of his bodies.

---

1. https://books2read.com/u/3LdnrX

2. https://books2read.com/u/3LdnrX